DRAW AlphaBeasts

130+ MONSTERS, ALIENS AND ROBOTS FROM LETTERS AND NUMBERS

steve HARPSTER

IMPACT
CINCINNATI, OHIO
IMPACTUniverse.com

Contents

Grab your pencil

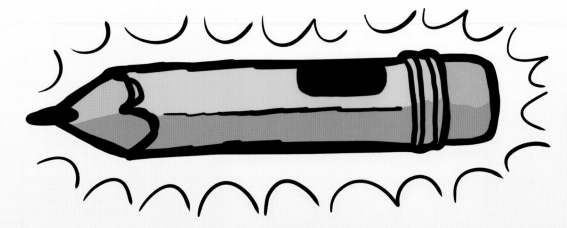

and your paper

and turn on your . . .

imagination!

In this book you're going to . . .

draw awesome aliens . . .

render rad robots . . .

AWESOME ALIENS

Welcome to the far reaches of the galaxy, where aliens of all shapes and sizes live, work and play. Some are dangerous xenomorphs ready to take over planets. Others are lighthearted, friendly folks willing to lend a hand, claw or tentacle. Each alien is drawn starting with a number. Speaking of numbers, it's time to blast off! Three . . . two . . . one . . . see you on the next page!

Zug

Fweeg

Gurp

Korg

ART TIP

Aliens have many different skin types. They might have scales or bumps. Some are slimey, while others are covered in fur. When drawing aliens, think about the type of planet they live on and the skin that would best suit them for that world.

Zeep

Skreek

Durb

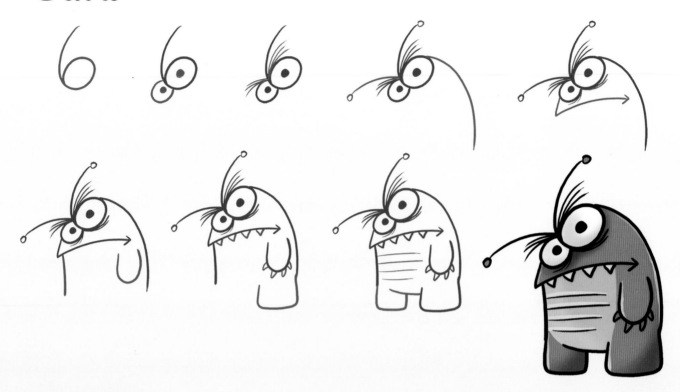

Zurgle

Sworp

Vormulac

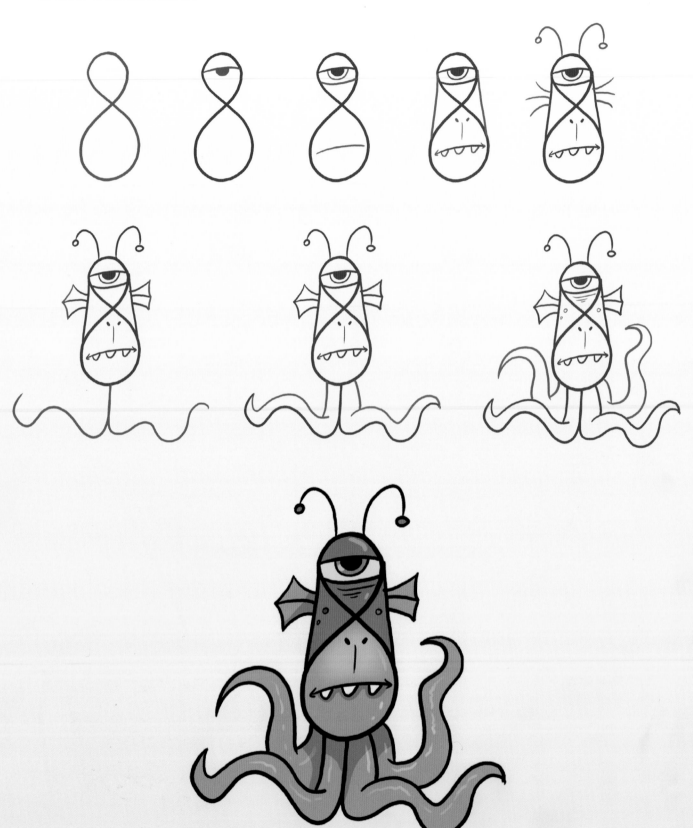

Slurg

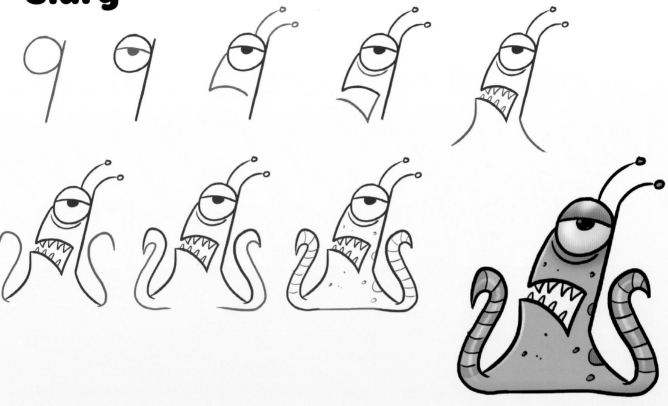

Hork

Durgle

Gorj

Zamulak

ART TIP

Space gear can be added to any of your aliens. Jet packs, helmets, gravity boots and utility belts are all the rage in space fashion. Try inventing some creative gadgets for aliens to wear.

Ramzor

Furp

Zick

Skork

Twip

Zargon

Ever try to scratch a bug bite while wearing a space suit?

ART TIP

Aliens can have three eyes and four arms or one big giant eye and no arms. Use the power of imagination to create all kinds of fun alien life forms.

Dr. Z

Skig

Ramptar

RAD ROBOTS

Hello human, we robots are excited to begin. Every robot starts out with a letter. Follow each step to the exact specifications to create the perfect robot friend. Or try making changes to the robots using that most interesting of human skills: imagination.

Copter Bot

Skark Bot

Blug Bot

Gurila

Arfy-22

Skram Bot

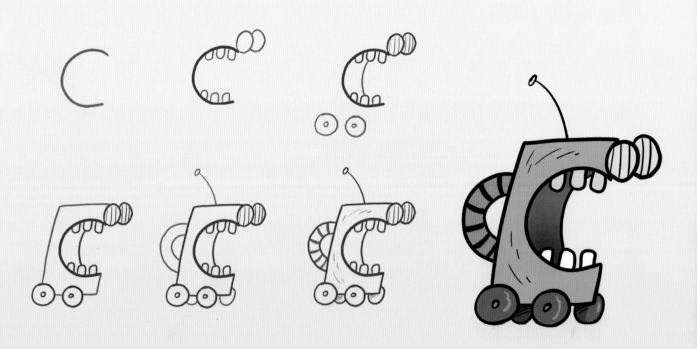

B-99

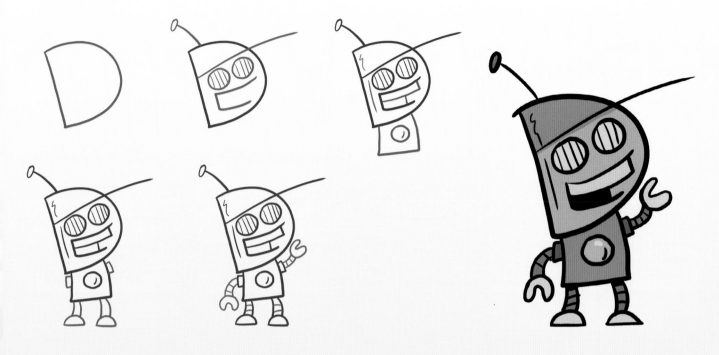

Bort

Hoover-23

ART TIP

Rivets, rust and dents are all a part of being a working bot. Robots might start off as clean sleek machines but over time they get scratched up and rusty. Try aging the robots with these different techniques.

- Broken eye panel
- Bent antennae
- Dents and scratches
- Metal plates bolted to body
- Replacement parts that don't match original

Trank

Robo-Rex

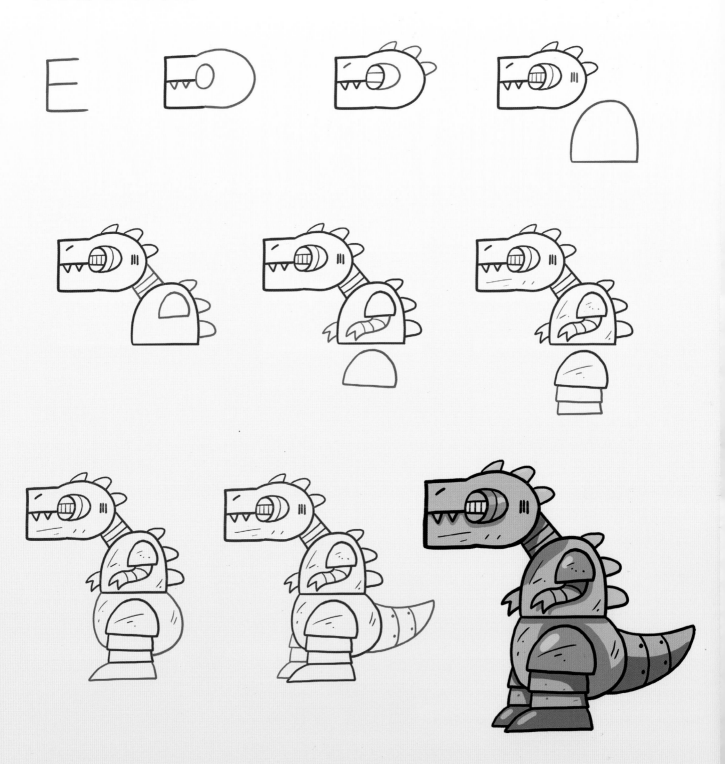

Crusher-99

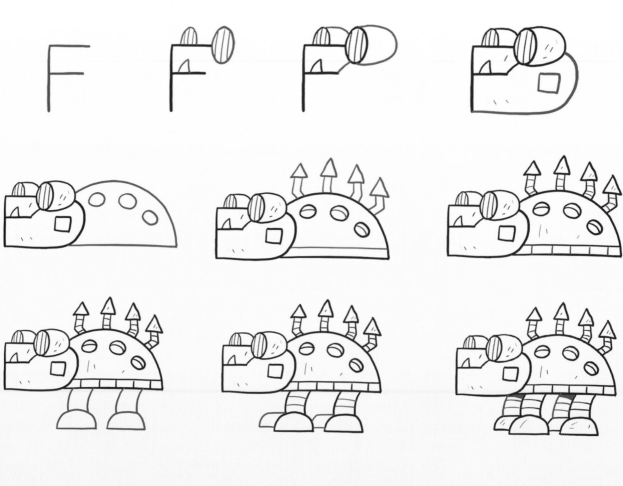

Chomp Bot

Kip

Q-68

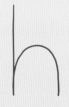 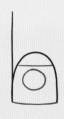 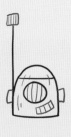 

Jlarg

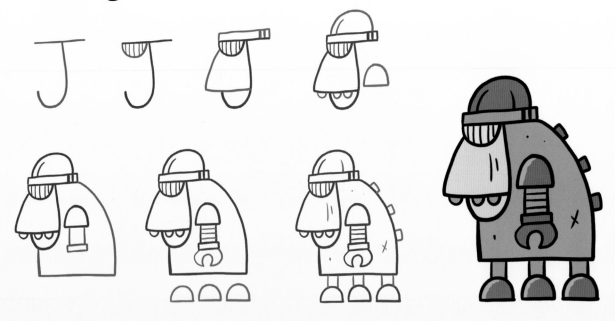

Krage

LG-38

TR-55

R-9-O

Kip Bot

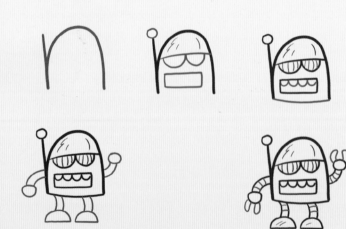

RB-33

RV-12

D-Structor

Scooby

Kronk

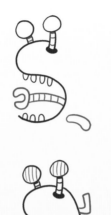

RGB-88

U-R-99

VIC-TOR

Kiwkz

55-38

Skig

DJ-96

G8TR

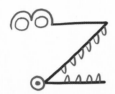  

DANGER! DO NOT TURN TO THE NEXT PAGE. MONSTER LIFE FORMS HAVE BEEN DETECTED.

MONSTER MAYHEM

Do not worry, artist, we monsters are very friendly. We love drawing and painting and making messes. Have fun drawing us, and do not worry about making mistakes. We live in an imaginary world, so there is no right or wrong when drawing a monster.

* Drawings on the wall were created by Tyler and Cooper Harpster.

Arrg

Blarg

Crug

Carbog

Dun-Dog

Dirge

ART TIP

Look at these different monster faces. Notice that each face is the same, but the eye is different. Just by changing the eye, you create an entirely new look, mood and expression.

Egard

Fang

Grub

Horace

Horton

Igle

Jub-Jub

Kogar

Klorn

Leech

Mort

Ness E

Ooozle

Opto

Plug

ART TIP

Feel free to explore changing these cute, lovable monsters into nightmare-fueled, bad-breathed beasts of rage.

80

Quig

Rock

Snarg

Sluggo

Tork

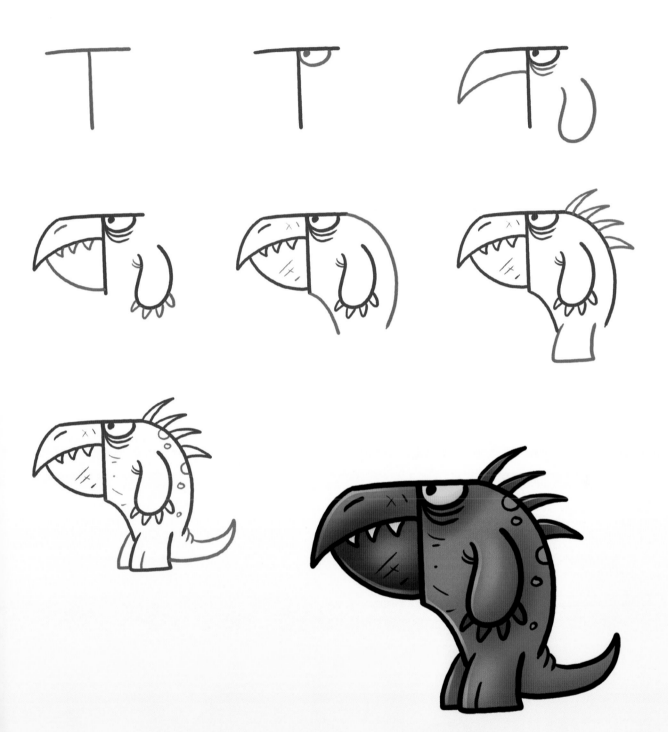

Urp

Vurg

Warg

88

Wyatt

Xark

Xog

Yuk

Zerk

HAUNTED CREEPS OF SPIDERBITE HOUSE

Good evening artists, and welcome to Spiderbite, home to many strange and mysterious creatures. Zombies roam the property, and skeletons may pop up from beneath the ground. The swamp is protected by many a monster, and the garden might eat you alive. Have fun touring the Spiderbite House, but be careful—many people have entered but no one has ever escaped!

Igg

Crash

Chuck the Zombie

Arthur the Werewolf

Dave the Swamp Creature

Bad Bill

Anthony

Xavier Owl

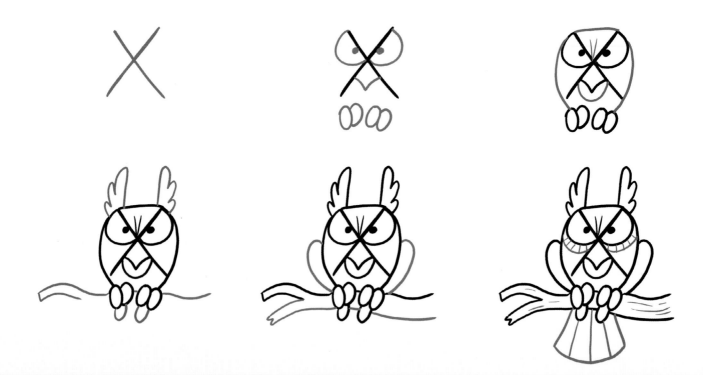

Randy

Norbert

Lady Lenor

Mortimer

Killer Plant

Screaming Squash

Putrid Mushroom

Growling Lion Plant

Quick Bite Plant

Eater Plant

Tiger Flower

Chomper Bee

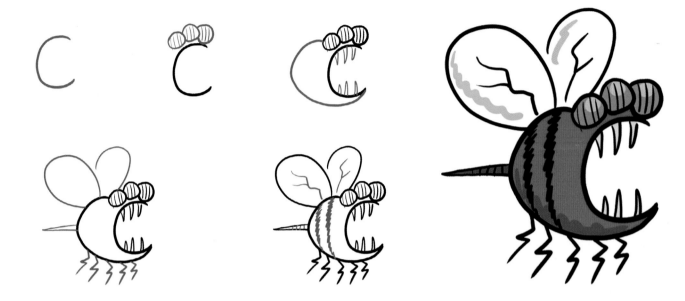

Root Bug

Bitey

Freddy Bones

Yug

Jasper

Zip

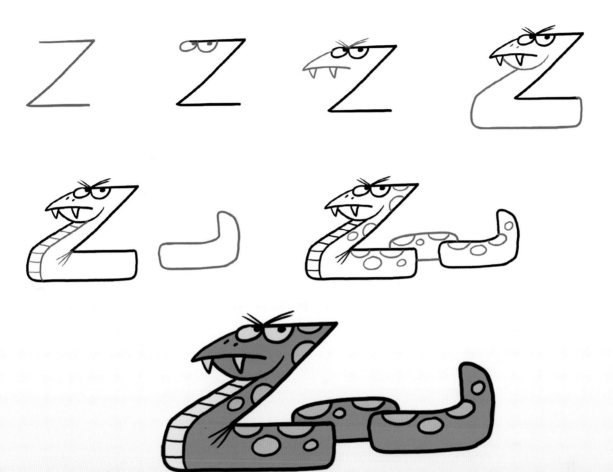

ART TIPS

The drawings in this book are simple, but add some details and see how the drawing changes. Do this to other drawings in this book to see how simple becomes complex.

Hank

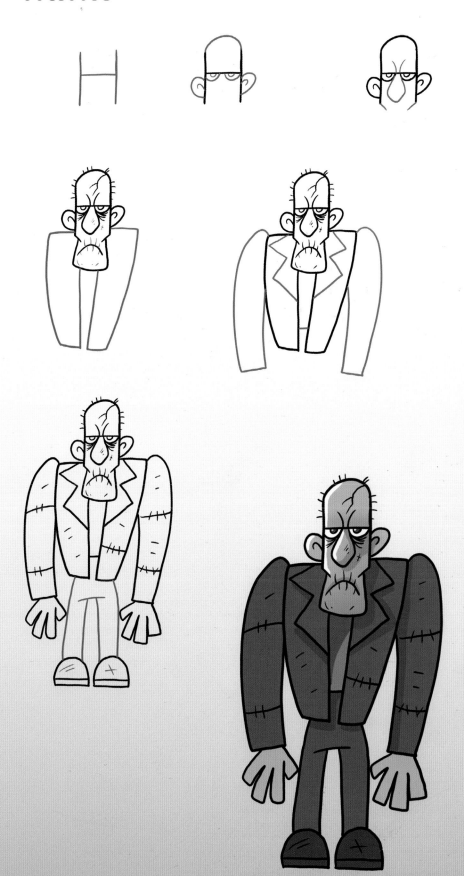

The R.I.P. Roadster

Eddie Ecto Goo

Chef Gunk

Jurg

Plurk

ART TIPS

Need a character to look the other direction? Just flip the letter or number backwards and try drawing it flipped. It might take some work, but it can be done.

Dr. Tinkor

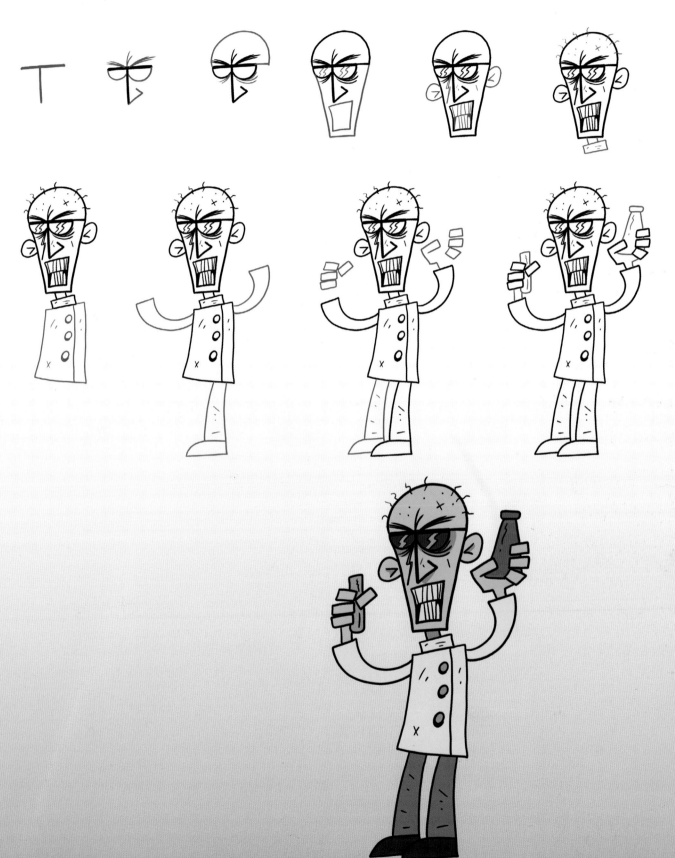

Vlad Bat

Urkle

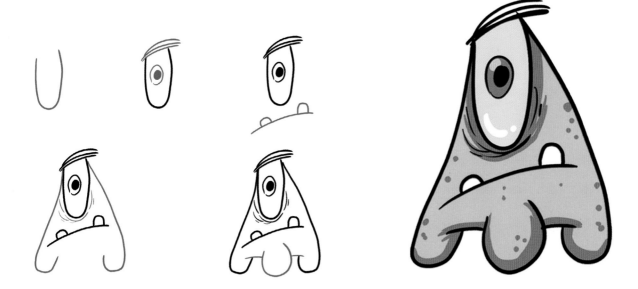

Zork

Rat

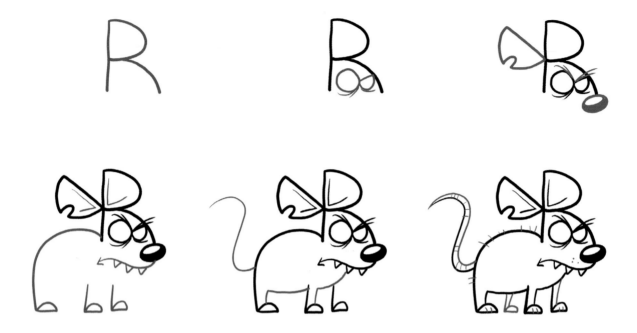

Skug Bug

ART TIPS

Try creating characters using letters: It's easy. Draw the eyes on a letter and see what happens.

B N Z

Oliver

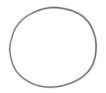

CREATE YOUR OWN ALPHABEASTS HERE!

ABOUT THE AUTHOR

Steve Harpster has authored and illustrated more than ninety books for children, and his artwork can be found on a variety of products such as T-shirts, stickers, toys and games. In 2010 Harpster created a company called Harptoons with the goal of getting children to draw, create and imagine. Through his books, videos and school visits, Harpster hopes to encourage children to create their own books, characters, worlds and video games.

Harpster resides in Cincinnati, Ohio, with his wife and two sons, Tyler and Cooper. When Harpster isn't busy drawing or visiting schools, he likes to watch movies, play with his kids and ride roller coasters. His favorite foods are pizza and burgers, and his favorite dessert is ice cream or anything chocolate.

See more of Harpster's work at Harptoons.com or at his Facebook page, Harptoons Publishing.

Watch Harpster's how-to-draw videos on YouTube at Steve Harpster or Harptoons.

DEDICATION AND ACKNOWLEDGMENTS

First, I want to thank my many drawing fans all over the world for their support. The many letters, emails and artwork sent by my fans have inspired me to keep on creating books, videos and art. Thank you from the bottom of my heart.

I would like to thank my parents for the love and support they gave me. They taught me how to work hard, set goals, stay optimistic through the hard times and level-headed during the good times.

My boys, Tyler and Cooper, deserve big thanks for keeping me on my toes and keeping a big smile on my face. Thank you for the many laughs, many hugs and many excuses to stop working to play. They also drew some of the art on pages 54 and 55 of this book. Thanks, boys!

Lastly, a thank you to my wife Karen for her grace and charm. She is always happy to take the kids out to give me more time to work. She helps me stay sane when I am completely crazy. She loves me when I am unlovable and forgives me for being the crazy artist who tries too hard and takes on (and expects) too much. Thanks for sticking with me, Boo!

Metric Conversion Chart

To convert	to	multiply by
Inches	Centimeters	2.54
Centimeters	Inches	0.4
Feet	Centimeters	30.5
Centimeters	Feet	0.03
Yards	Meters	0.9
Meters	Yards	1.1

a content + ecommerce company

Other fine IMPACT books are available from your favorite bookstore, art supply store or online supplier. Visit our website at fwmedia.com.

22 21 20 19 18 5 4 3 2 1

DISTRIBUTED IN THE U.K. AND EUROPE
BY F&W MEDIA INTERNATIONAL LTD
Pynes Hill Court, Pynes Hill, Rydon Lane, Exeter,
EX2 5AZ, United Kingdom
Tel: (+44) 1392 79680
Email: enquiries@fwmedia.com

ISBN 13: 978-1-4403-5404-5

Edited by Jennifer Zellner
Cover designed by Jamie Olson
Interior and back cover designed by Alex Doherty
Production coordinated by Debbie Thomas

IDEAS. INSTRUCTION. INSPIRATION.

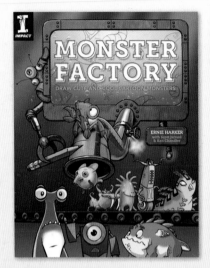

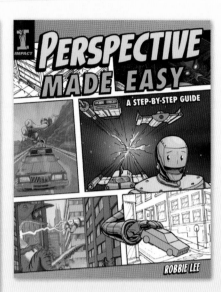

Check out these IMPACT titles at IMPACTUniverse.com!

These and other fine IMPACT products are available at your local art & craft retailer, bookstore or online supplier. Visit our website at IMPACTUniverse.com.

Follow IMPACT for the latest news, free wallpapers, free demos and chances to win FREE BOOKS!

Follow us!

IMPACTUNIVERSE.COM

- Connect with your favorite artists
- Get the latest in comic, fantasy and sci-fi art instruction, tips and techniques
- Be the first to get special deals on the products you need to improve your art